DAVE MARTONE'S

Serious Shred

GET YOUR FINGERS TO PLAY
WHAT'S IN YOUR HEAD

Alfred Music Publishing Co., Inc.
P.O. Box 10003
Van Nuys, CA 91410-0003
alfred.com

ISBN-10: 0-7390-8610-3 (Book & DVD)
ISBN-13: 978-0-7390-8610-0 (Book & DVD)

Cover guitar courtesy of Ibanez Guitars (Hoshino USA)
Author photo courtesy of Dave Martone

 Alfred Cares. Contents printed on 100% recycled paper.

Contents

TUNE UP

In the DVD menu, select Tuning. It will take you to a page where you will hear an audio track that will play each string several times, starting with the 1st string, high E. Compare your strings to this audio track to get in tune with the DVD.

A NOTE ABOUT THE VIDEO

The DVD video corresponds to lessons in the book and the two are intended to be used together. For lessons that use Jam Tracks, go to the DVD menu and select Jam Tracks, where you can access the tracks that correspond with specific lessons. The video lessons included on this DVD were filmed at various times over the period of a year; thus, you will note wardrobe and lighting changes from lesson to lesson.

Introduction

If you have been playing long enough to feel limited by what you know and what your fingers can do, the Serious Shred DVDs and books are for you. You have developed some lead guitar chops and know some scales and lots of chords, but would like to be able to play like the killer shredders you have heard. Each DVD/book combination in this series features a monster shredder guitarist teaching the left- and/or right-hand techniques and musical concepts you need to master to become the shredder you want to be. You'll be learning from the best, and will be inspired by the amazing demonstrations of licks and exercises in the video.

The optimum learning experience with the Serious Shred DVD/book series is to watch the video, guitar in hand ready to play, with the book open in front of you. Numbers will be displayed on your television or computer screen, directing you to licks and exercises in the book that include standard music notation, TAB, and chord or scale fretboard diagrams. Stop the video any time you need to practice an example. To ensure the effectiveness of the training offered here, master each lick or exercise before continuing on to the next lesson.

To make it easier for you to choose the appropriate Serious Shred DVD and book, they have been categorized into levels that are explained below.

ESSENTIAL
This level assumes you can read TAB and/or standard music notation, and know how to read chord and scale fretboard diagrams. You know all of the basic open-position chords and are ready for barres and other movable chords. You have some familiarity with the pentatonic scale, and are ready to learn a number of alternate positions in which it can be played. You're ready to master fundamental techniques like hammer-ons, pull-offs, alternate picking, and even some more specialized techniques, such as palm muting, bending, legato, vibrato, fingerstyle, tapping, and sweep picking. You also have the music theory background needed to begin learning the modes of the major scale and incorporate them into your soloing.

ADVANCED
To begin at this level, you should have all of the skills and knowledge developed at the ESSENTIAL level and are ready to explore more advanced techniques and concepts. You have the musical understanding needed to learn all the different types of 7th chords, plus extended and altered chords in a variety of voicings. You're ready for advanced applications of sweeping, tapping, harmonics, and whammy bar techniques. Your ready to explore topics such as phrasing, multi-finger tapping, Hendrix-style chord embellishments, and more.

ABOUT DAVE MARTONE

Dave Martone is a guitarist, composer, and educator who has worked with such luminaries as Joe Satriani, Jennifer Batten, Paul Gilbert, Yngwie Malmsteen, Marty Friedman, Seymour Duncan, Greg Howe, Mike Portnoy, and more.

Martone has been featured in *Guitar Player* magazine and also in *Guitar One* magazine, where he was named one of the top four underground shredders in North America.

Martone endorses Vox, Digitech, Parker, Cakewalk, GHS, and Radial Engineering. For more about Dave Martone, check out: www.davemartone.com

Blues Scales Lesson 1: Connecting Boxes

(Important note: Throughout this book, I will refer to pentatonic and blues scale "boxes" and "shapes"—these terms are interchangeable. On page 44, you will find the pentatonic and blues scale boxes used in this book. Please check these out now if you are unfamiliar with them, or refer to them when needed.)

So, we all have the problem of being stuck in one box shape while playing blues scales. In this lesson, we'll go through three exercises to help break this bad habit. All of these exercises will go through a three-string sequence, then slide into the next box, and all of these licks will be in the key of F♯ Minor or A Major. Our goal in this lesson is to break out of the traditional blues box shapes to connect to their neighboring patterns on the fretboard. There are many ways to do this, including the slide technique, which is what we will be using.

CONNECTING BOXES 1, 2, AND 3

We'll start by playing Box 1 on the bottom three strings, then slide into Box 2. Next, we'll slide from the 5th to the 7th fret on the 2nd string, which will take us to Box 3. Notice that the fingering pattern in each octave is the same. Let's try it.

Okay, now play it with some speed.

Let's play it backwards now, slowly at first.

Now, try the lick a little faster.

Connecting Boxes 2, 3, and 4

Now, we're going to connect Boxes 2, 3, and 4 using the same three-string shape idea as above.

We'll start in Box 2 (which could be thought of as a *major blues scale* if we were designating A as our tonic) and, again, slide into Box 3 on the 4th string, where we will repeat the fingering pattern we just played on the bottom three strings.

Then, a slide on the 2nd string will take us into Box 4, where we will repeat the fingering pattern played in the previous two octaves.

Let's try the whole lick, slowly at first.

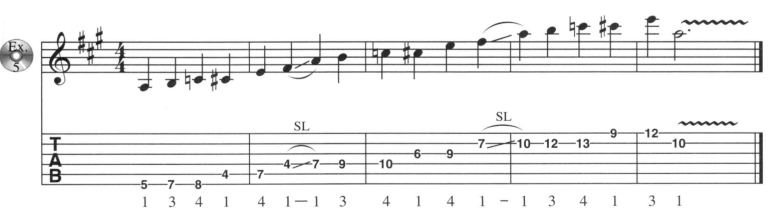

Now, with a bit more juice.

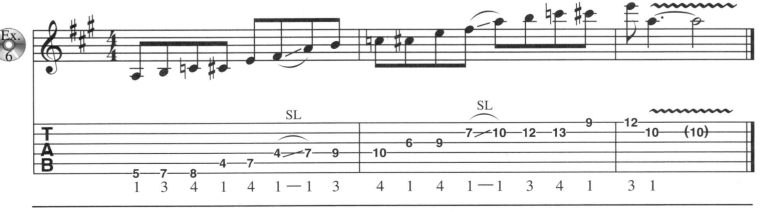

Now, of course, we have to play it backwards. Always remember to try your ideas backwards; this will double the number of licks in your arsenal. Play the following slowly.

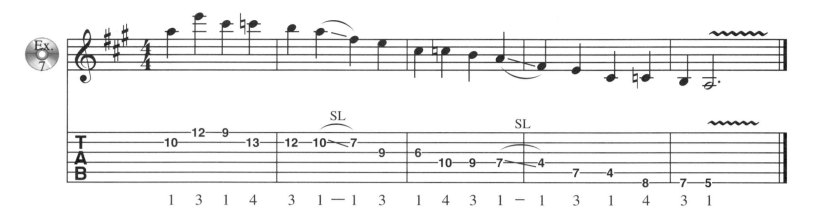

Now, try it with a bit more speed.

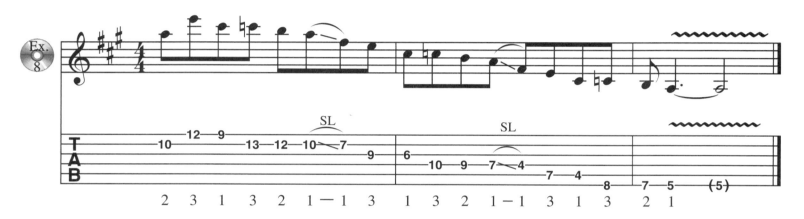

CONNECTING BOXES 3, 4, AND 5

For the final part of this lesson, we'll be connecting Boxes 3, 4, and 5 using the same idea as the previous two sections.

Starting in Box 3, play the three-string pattern and slide up to the 9th fret on the 4th string; this takes us into Box 4. Proceed by playing the same shape as the previous octave, sliding on the 2nd string into Box 5.

Let's try it slowly.

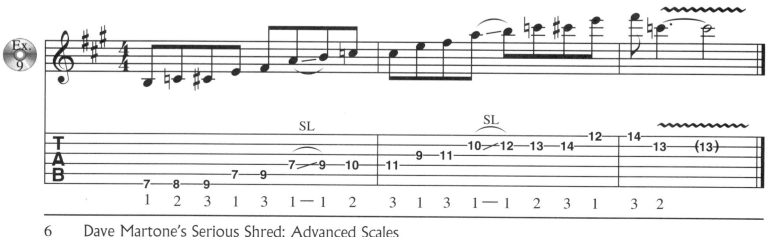

Now, let's rip it up a little bit.

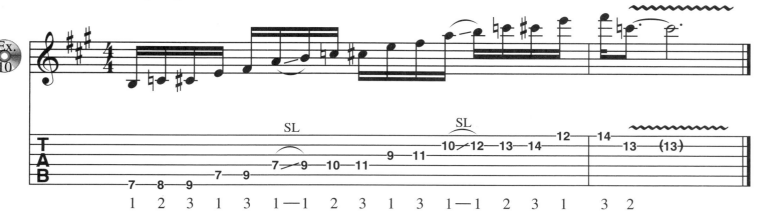

As always, let's try this idea backwards—slowly at first.

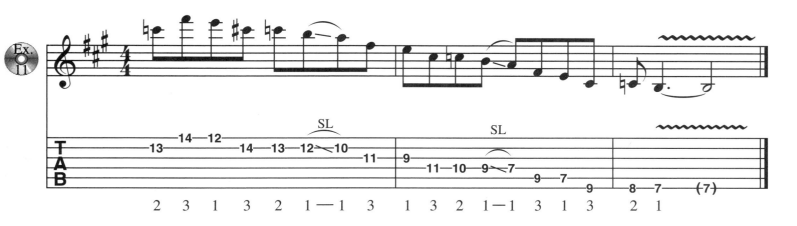

Now, play it a little faster.

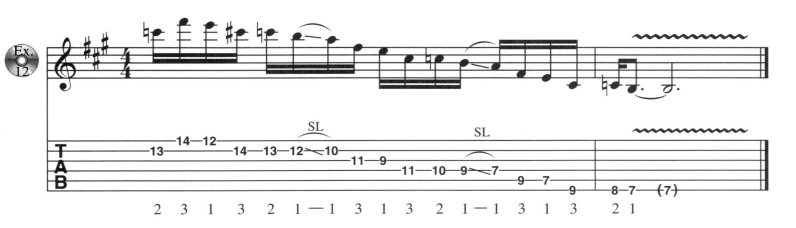

You just learned how to connect the various blues scale boxes using the concept of a three-string fingering pattern that repeats in each new octave. Work on these ideas until you have mastered them.

Blues Scales Lesson 2: Two-String Patterns

Okay, most of you like playing three-note-per-string scale patterns, I assume. Well, this lesson will not disappoint you. We'll connect the box shapes for a massive three-octave blues scale. Keep in mind that these three-note-per-string patterns will require some stretching of your fretting hand.

LICK NO. 1: THREE NOTES PER STRING

In the previous lesson, we used three-string shapes; here, we'll use two-string shapes. See the fretboard diagram below the music for an illustration of the repeating two-string shape. We'll start with the lick **A**, do variation **B** and then speed it up.

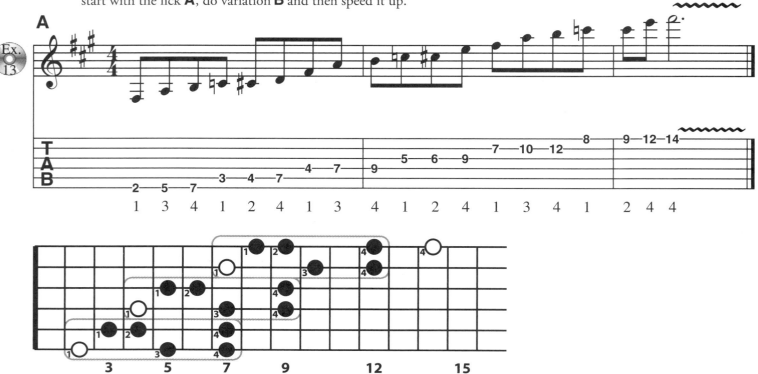

LICK NO. 1 VARIATION

Following is a variation of Lick No. 1. Just play every two-string pattern ascending, descending, and ascending again—and end with a whole-step bend at the 12th fret of the 1st string.

Practice the whole lick slowly at first, then bring it up to tempo.

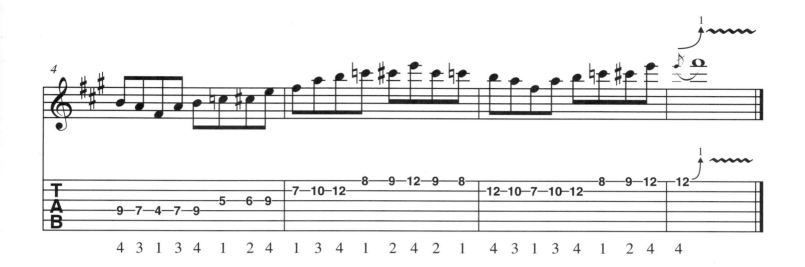

Now, let's try this variation with a little more juice.

LICK NO. 2: THREE OCTAVES FROM BOX 2

We're going to start from Box 2 on A. Again, you could think of this as the major blues scale form. The same two-string pattern is played on strings 6 and 5, 4 and 3, and 2 and 1.

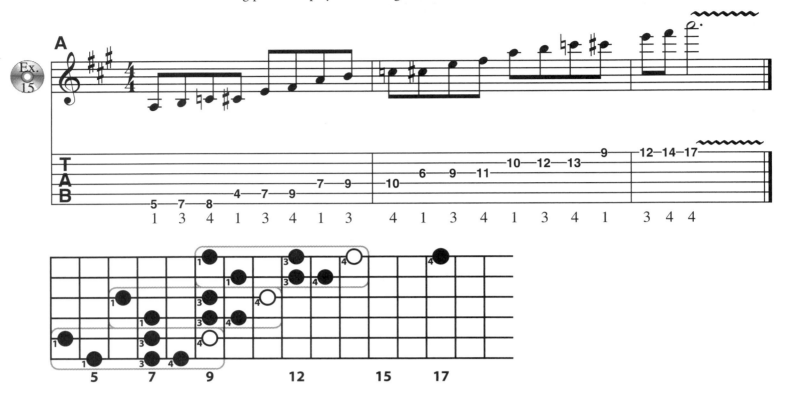

LICK NO. 2 VARIATION

Now, let's play a variation of the example above. It's the same idea as the Lick No. 1 Variation on page 8. Play the first module (two-string pattern) up, down, then up again. Then repeat this for the second and third modules. Let's try the whole thing, slowly first.

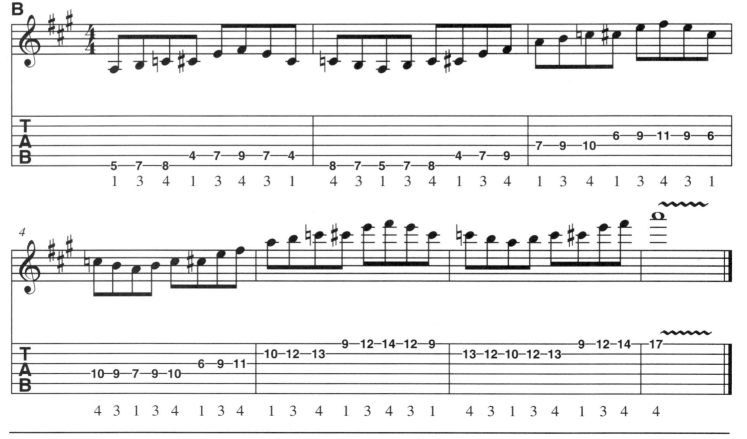

Great, now let's do it with some speed!

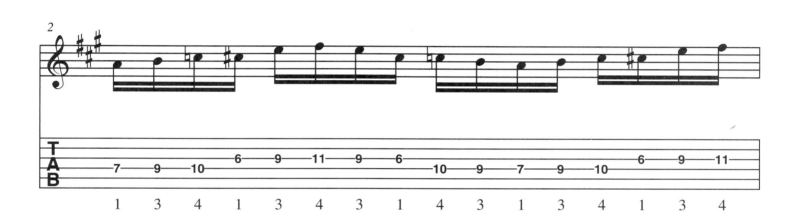

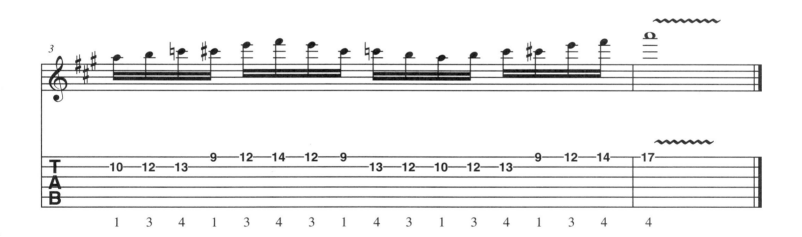

Make sure you are comfortable with the lick above before moving on to the next section.

LICK NO. 3: THREE OCTAVES FROM BOX 5

Now, it's time to move on to the higher frets. We'll be starting in Box 5 and working our way up
to the 24th fret, using our repeating two-string pattern idea. Try the following example slowly.

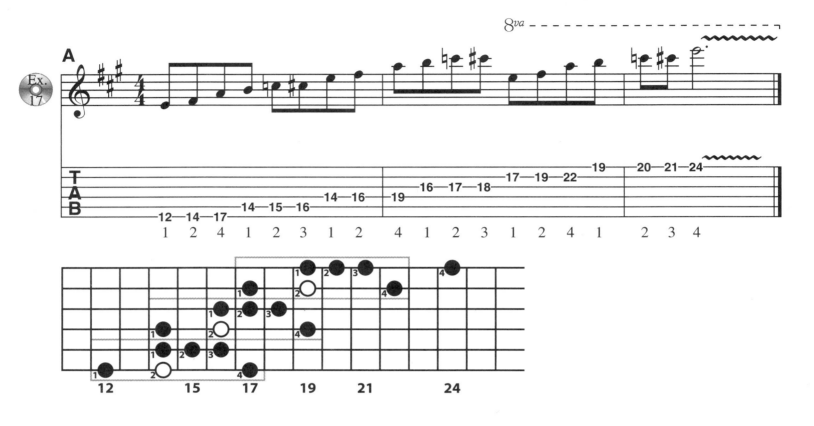

LICK NO. 3 VARIATION

Now, let's play a variation of the lick above—going up, down, then up again on each module.
Try the following example slowly at first.

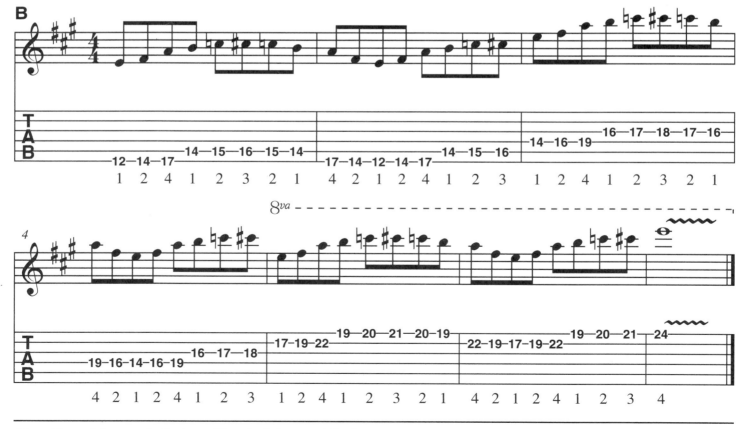

Now, let's play the variation faster.

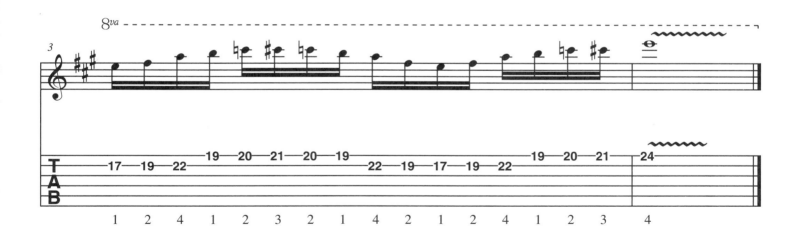

I hope you enjoyed this lesson. Now, you have the tools to create amazing blues-scale licks of your own!

Advanced Minor Scales and Modes: Lesson 1

This lesson prepares you to play the natural minor, or Aeolian, scale over the entire fretboard by using a few formulas and some patterns. We'll also work on accessing our relative major, which is an important part of this process. Let's get started.

D Aeolian Formula

The first thing we need to know is the simple formula to build this scale from any starting note (we'll be using D Minor in the following examples). In terms of steps, this formula is: whole–half–whole–whole–half–whole–whole (see below). This means that starting from the note D—anywhere on the fretboard—you can plug in that formula and get an Aeolian scale.

D Aeolian (Natural Minor)

Now, let's play the D Natural Minor scale over the entire fretboard. Start on D (6th string, 10th fret) and plug in the formula above. Then, do the same thing from another D (5th fret, 5th string), and another D (open 4th string), etc.

D Aeolian (Natural Minor) on Each String

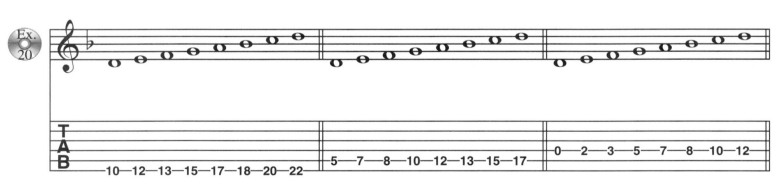

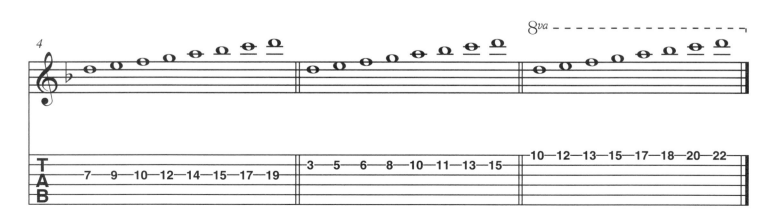

F Major Scale (Relative Major of D Natural Minor)

Now, let's look at the relative major of D Minor, which is one and a half steps up from D. That gives us F Major. It's basically the same scale as the Aeolian, but starting from the note F. If we get used to locating relative major and minor scales in this way, we'll fill in all the blank areas of the fretboard.

The major scale formula is: whole–whole–half–whole–whole–whole–half.

F Major Scale

The root (F) is 1½ steps higher than the root (D) of its relative minor scale.

Now, as we did for the D Aeolian scale on page 14, let's play the F Major scale on each string, across the entire fretboard.

F Major on Each String

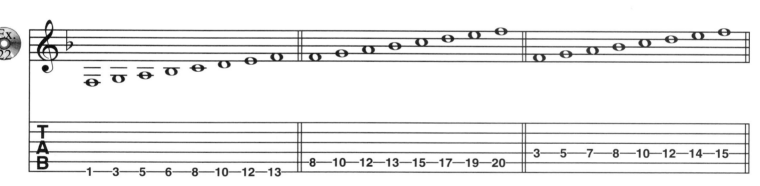

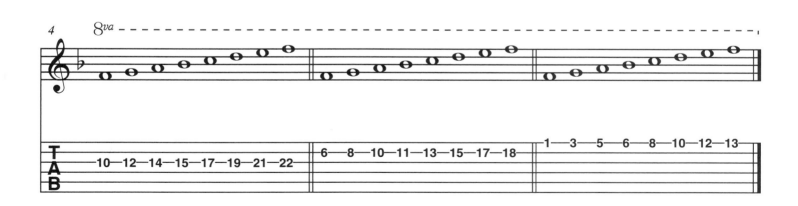

THREE-STRING MODAL PATTERNS

So far, we have learned the Aeolian and its relative major scale on every string. Now, we need to learn some patterns moving across the strings. In this lesson, we will look at seven patterns—all one-octave scales on strings 6, 5, and 4. Each will have a cool mode name that you might have heard before.

Let's start with the relative of D Minor, which is F Major, otherwise known as F Ionian. Next is G Dorian, then A Phrygian, B♭ Lydian, C Mixolydian, D Aeolian (our key, or home scale), E Locrian, and back to F Ionian. Remember that all of these patterns can be used over a D Minor chord, as they all use the same notes. Let's play them.

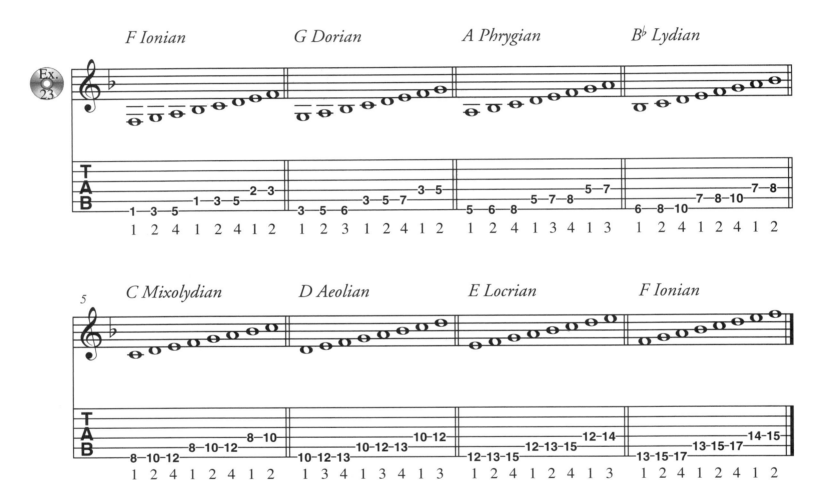

Now, let's play through all of the patterns together.

THE MOTHER LODE: SEVEN SIX-STRING MODAL PATTERNS

Now, we get to the mother lode of all seven patterns in a three-note-per-string sequence up the neck, which will enable us to play Aeolian anywhere on the fretboard. This part of the lesson expands on the previous patterns by adding the 3rd, 2nd, and 1st strings. Check out the following diagrams and play all of the shapes ascending and descending.

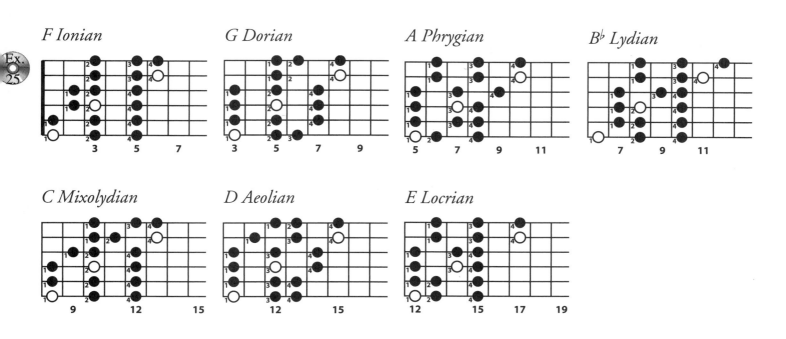

Playing All Seven Six-String Modal Patterns

How do you feel after all that work? Tired? I hope not, because it's time to make music! On the video, we'll be playing over a backing track consisting of the chords D Minor and C Major (see diagrams to the right). This progression outlines an Aeolian sound in the key of D Minor, or the relative F Major. We'll play all the box shapes ascending and descending, starting from F Major, all the way to the Locrian pattern. If all of these patterns are played over this progression, everything will sound Aeolian.

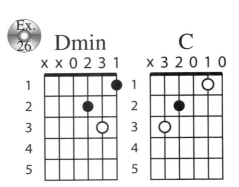

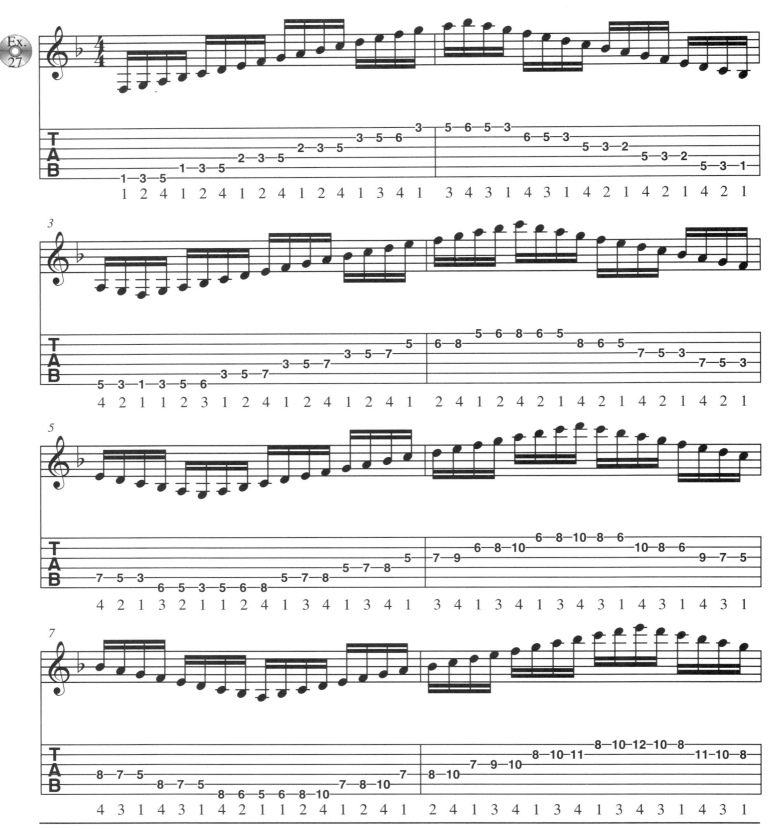

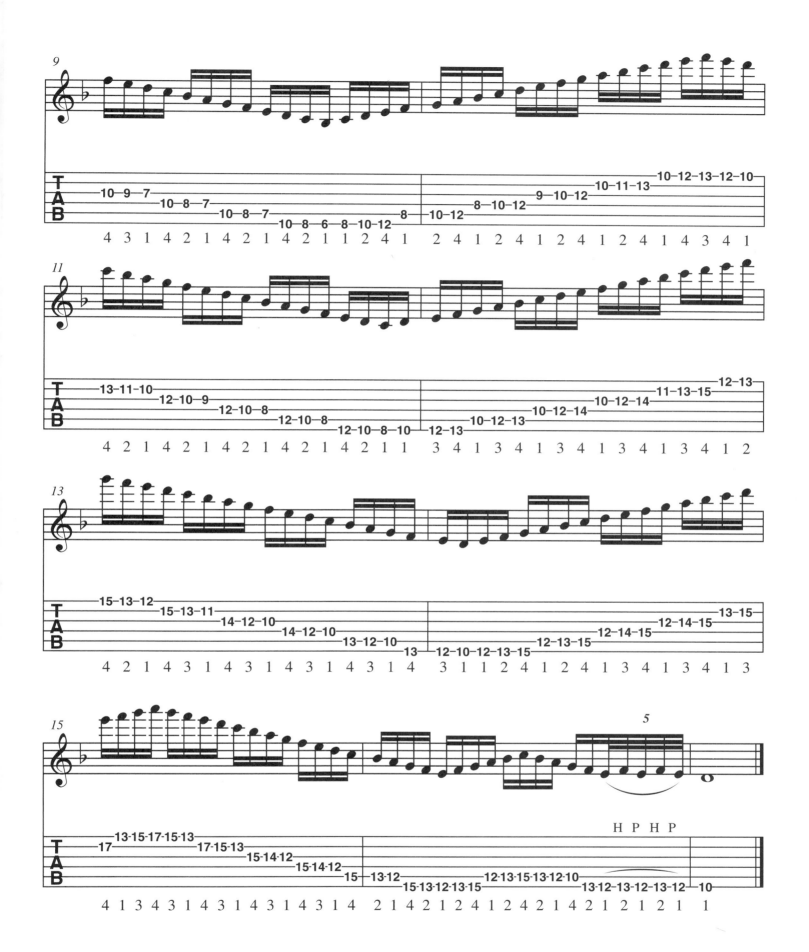

Take your time and work hard to master these patterns before moving on to the next lesson.

Advanced Minor Scales and Modes: Lesson 2

Since we have learned the Aeolian mode across the neck, it is a simple task to now do the same with the Dorian mode.

G Dorian Formula

Our first concept to understand is that if we start any major scale from the second note, we get a Dorian scale. So, if we play G Dorian (starting from the second note of the F Major scale), the step formula is: whole–half–whole–whole–whole–half–whole.

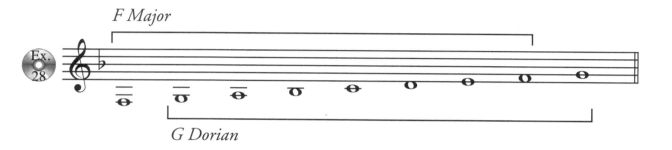

Now, let's play G Dorian, then the F Major scale (from which G Dorian is derived), then D Aeolian. Notice the same notes exist in all three scales.

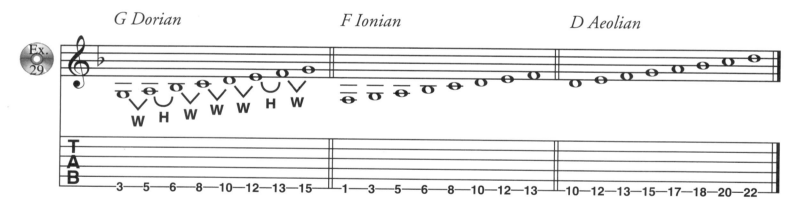

Now for the secret: It's the chords we play that outline the sound of the scale, just as with our last lesson on the Aeolian mode. We'll get more into this in the next section, but for now, realize that all the scales we learned on one string are relative to each other.

Playing G Dorian

So, are you confused yet? I hope not, but if you are, this next section will help. Let us first play the Dorian shape from the note G on the 6th string. Play along with me to the backing track on the video, which is made up of only the second chord in the key of F—G Minor (Gmin). As you play, listen to the tonality of the scale. (Note: The example appears in standard music notation and TAB at the top of the next page.)

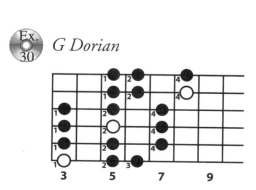

G Dorian

Now, let's play the F Ionian scale in the position of the key, which would be on the first note F at the 1st fret. Play this scale with me over the same backing track as above and listen to the tonality.

Okay, what did you notice about the last two examples? I hope you heard that they sounded pretty much the same except for the starting note. That's the point I'm trying to make. Many guitarists only know how to play the Dorian shape right on top of the root of the chord. But we have all the other shapes, modes, or boxes to play all over the neck. This idea works with all the boxes and modes.

DORIAN DOMINATION

Our next backing track consists of the chords G Minor 7 and C9. (Note: this is available on your DVD as a separate jam track.) These chords both come from the key of F Major. The G is the second chord in the key and C is the fifth chord in the key. This is a great Dorian progression for you to jam on. All we need to know is where all of our scales start. Remember that Dorian is just the major scale starting on the second note, and in the key of F Major, the 2nd note is G.

We're going to play through the entire modal pattern from F Major to E Locrian. When we play these scales over the G Minor 7 to C9 progression, we get a Dorian sound across the entire fretboard.

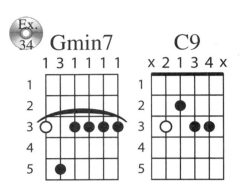

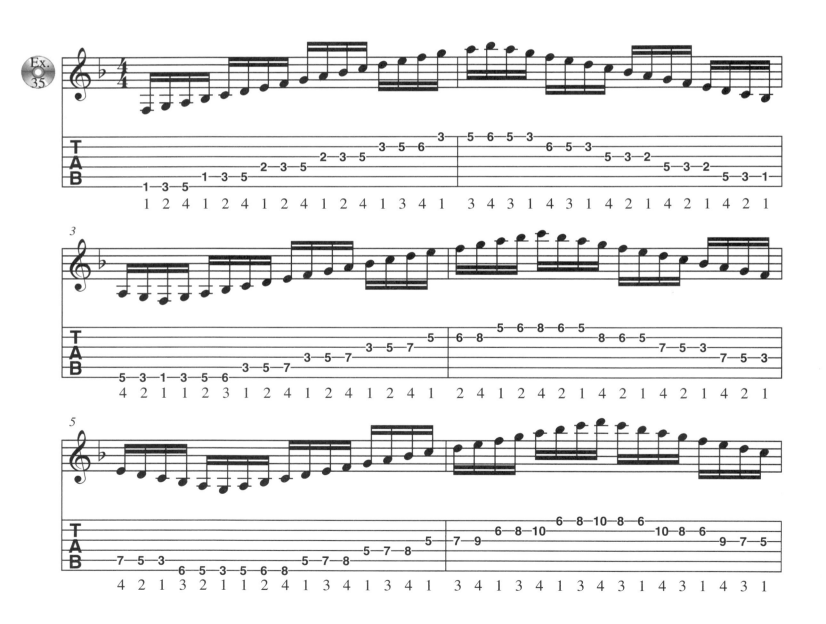

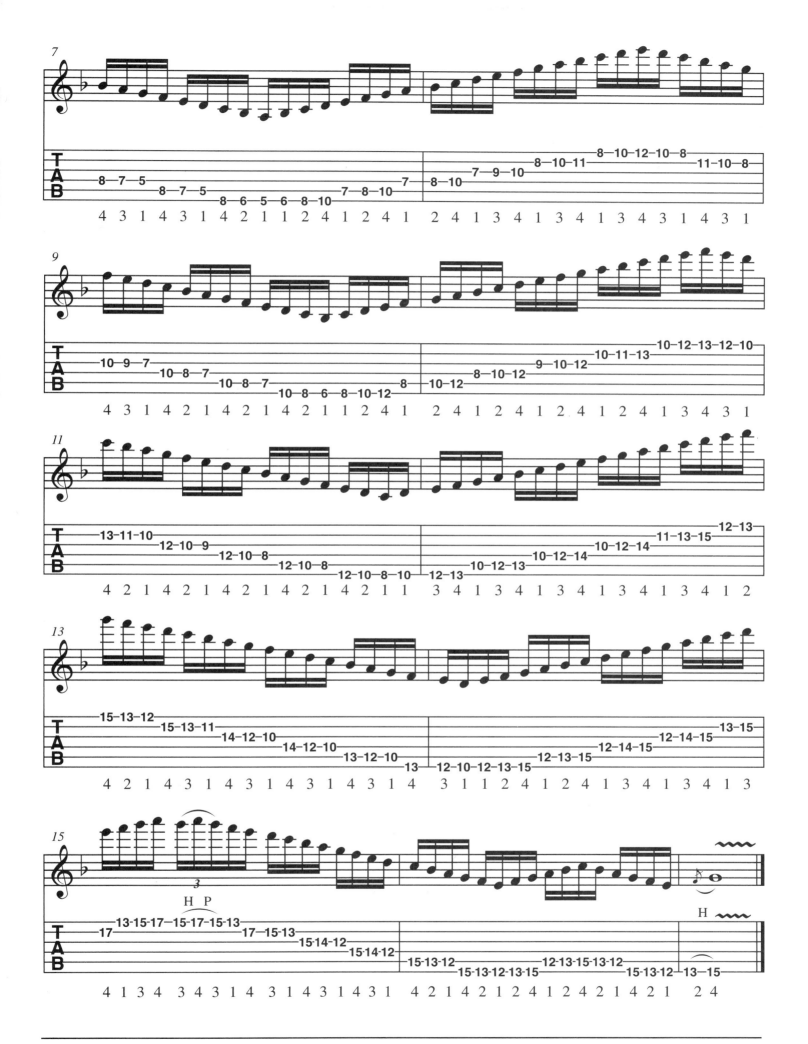

Since we have learned the Aeolian and Dorian modes across the neck, let's do the same with the Phrygian mode. Believe it or not, you already know how to do this! As long as you understood and mastered the last lesson, this lesson will be easy for you. Remember that by looking at the same scales in different ways, we can achieve great results.

A Phrygian Formula

Phrygian is the third mode of the major scale. So, if we start any major scale from the 3rd note, we get the Phrygian scale. The step formula for the Phrygian scale is: half–whole–whole–whole–half–whole–whole.

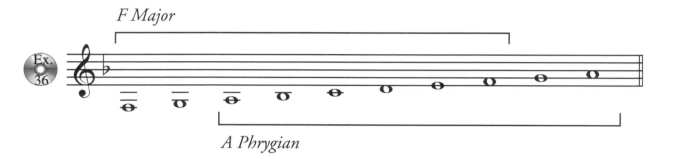

Now, let's play A Phrygian, then the F Major scale (from which A Phrygian is derived), then G Dorian. Notice the same notes exist in all three scales.

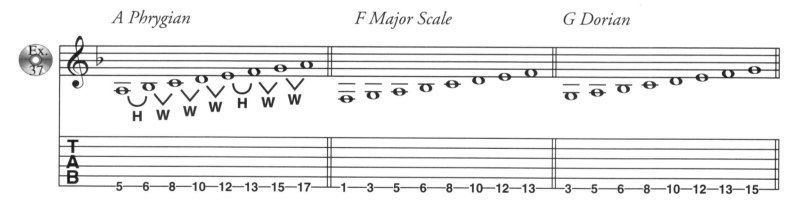

Remember, it's the chords we play that outline the sound of our scale, just as in our last lesson on the Dorian mode. Also, keep in mind that all the scales we just learned on one string are relative to each other.

Playing A Phrygian

Let's start by playing the Phrygian shape from the note A on the 6th string. Play along with me to the backing track on the video, which is made up of only the third chord in the key of F—A Minor (Amin). As you play, listen to the tonality of the scale. (Note: The example appears in standard music notation and TAB at the top of the next page.)

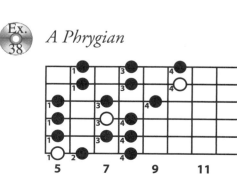

Ex. 38 *A Phrygian*

Now, let's play the F Ionian scale in the position of the key, which would be on the first note F at the 1st fret. Let's play this scale over the same backing track as above and listen to the tonality.

Okay, I hope you noticed that the last two examples sounded pretty much the same except for the starting note. Now, you won't be limited to playing the Phrygian shape right on the root of the chord—you have all the other shapes or boxes to play across the fretboard.

PHRYGIAN FREAK-OUT!

Now, we will do as we did in the Dorian lesson. Play along with me to the backing track on the video, which is made up of two chords from the key of F: A Minor and B♭ Major. A Minor is the third chord of the key and B♭ is the fourth chord of the key. This is a great Phrygian progression for you to jam on (and you can do this along with the separate jam track on your DVD). All we need to know is where to start all of our scales. Remember that Phrygian is just the major scale starting on the 3rd note. What we're going to do is play the entire modal pattern from F Major to E Locrian. When these patterns are played over this chord progression, we get a Phrygian sound across the entire fretboard.

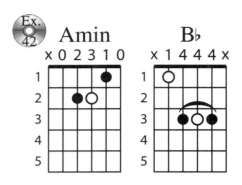

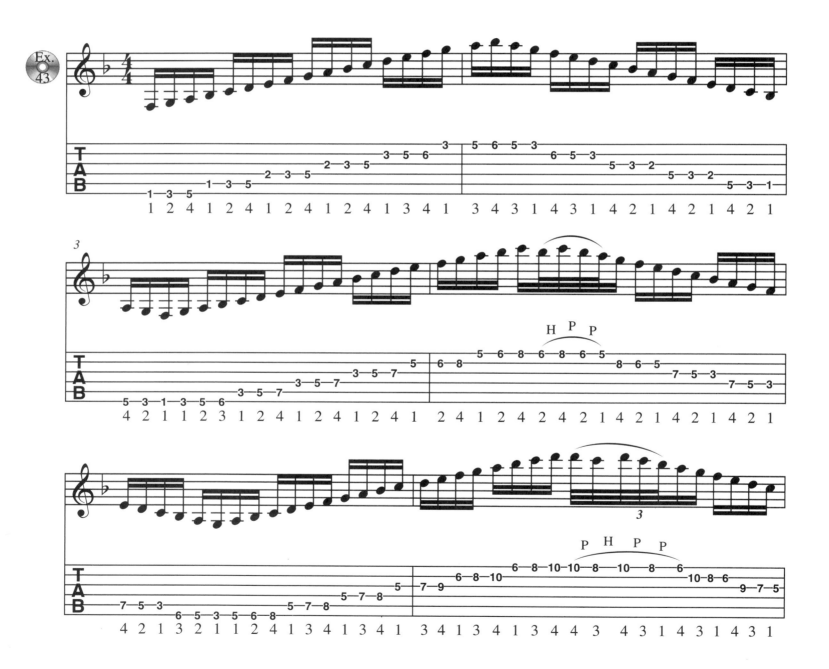

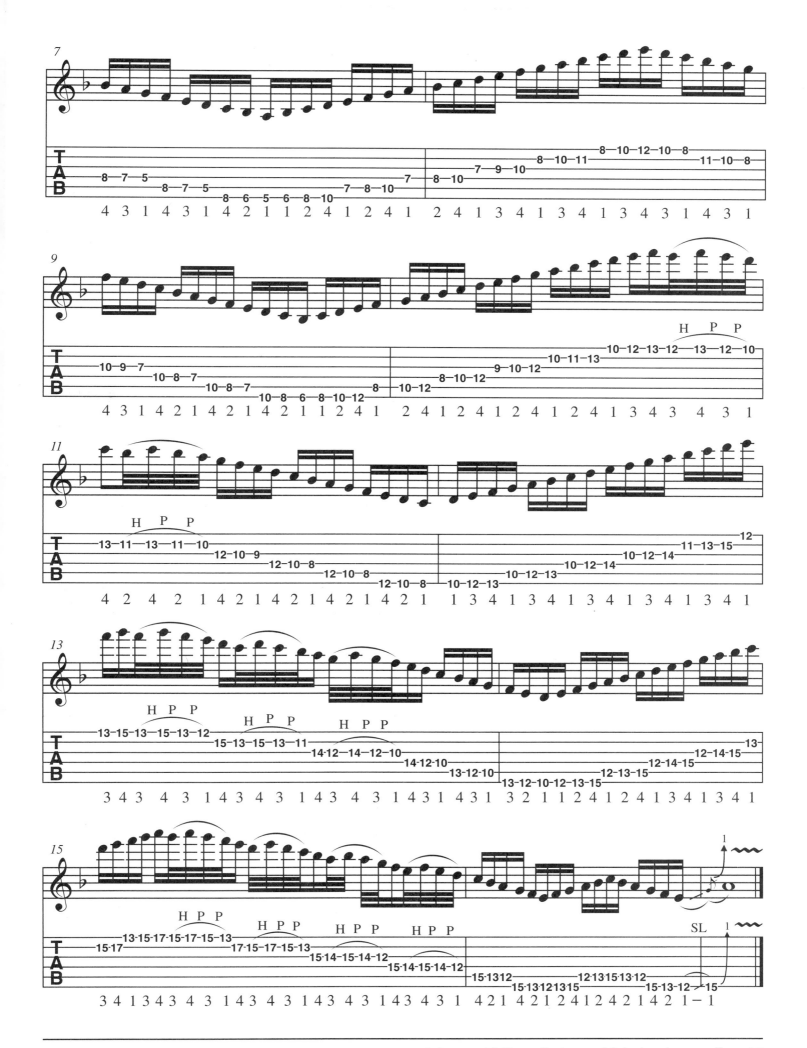

E Locrian Construction

Now, it's time to play the Locrian mode over the fretboard. Remember, Locrian is the seventh mode of the major scale, so if we were to start any major scale from the 7th note, we would get a Locrian scale. The step formula for Locrian is: half–whole–whole–half–whole–whole–whole.

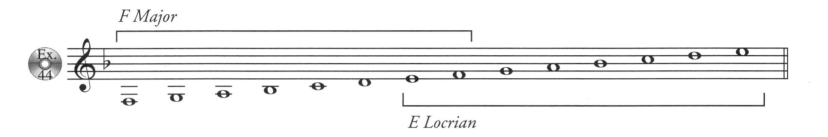

Now, let's play E Locrian, then the F Major scale (from which E Locrian is derived), then G Dorian. Notice the same notes exist in all three scales.

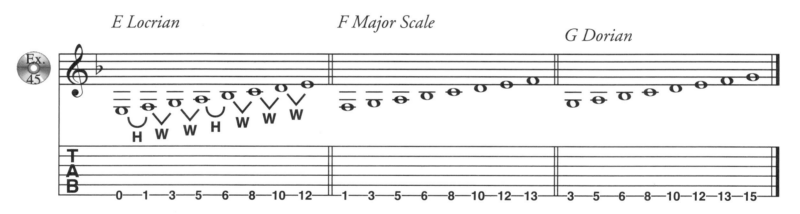

Remember, it's the chords we play that outline the sound of our scale, just as in our last lesson on the Phrygian mode.

Playing E Locrian

I know you have this stuff down now, so let's finish it off. Let's first play the simple Locrian shape in the diagram to your right. Then, play it along with me to the backing track on the video, which is made up only of the seventh chord in the key of F—Emin7♭5. As you play, listen to the tonality of the scale. (Note: The example appears in standard music notation and TAB at the top of the next page.)

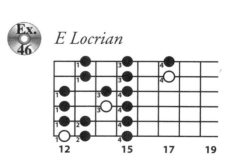

E Locrian

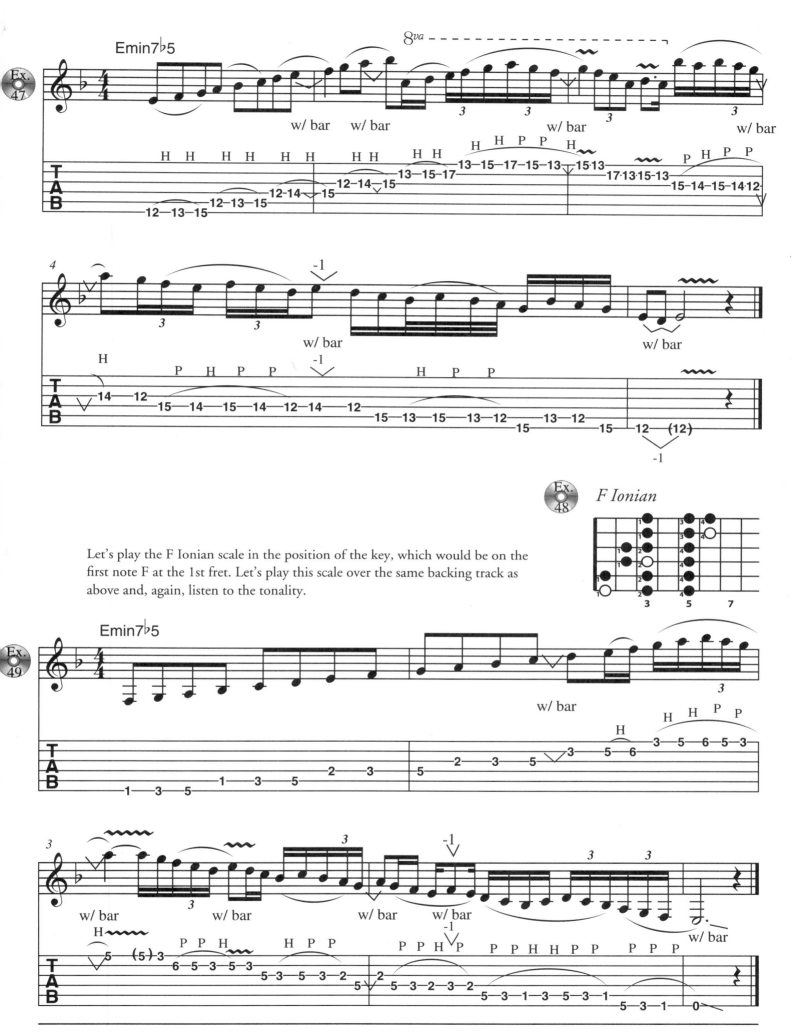

Let's play the F Ionian scale in the position of the key, which would be on the first note F at the 1st fret. Let's play this scale over the same backing track as above and, again, listen to the tonality.

Again, I'm sure you were able to notice that the two scales on the previous page sounded pretty much the same, except for the starting note. Now, you can play the Locrian shape across the entire fretboard using all of our other boxes, or modes.

LOCRIAN FINALE

All right, now that you're thoroughly familiar with all the boxes, it's time for you to jam on them in the Locrian mode. On the video, the backing track consists of the chords Emin7♭5 and Edim/A. Both of these chords come from the key of F Major: Emin7♭5 is the seventh chord in the key, and Edim is the triad 7th chord in the same key. This is a great Locrian progression for you to jam on (and you can do this along with the separate jam track on your DVD). All we need to know is where to start all of our scales. Remember that Locrian is just the major scale starting on the 7th note.

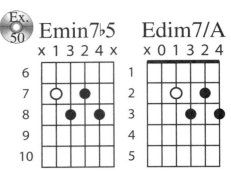

When improvising over the following chords, play through the entire modal progression starting on F Major and continuing through E Locrian. Over this chord progression, our modal patterns create a Locrian sound across the entire fretboard. (Note: Scale diagrams are under the example to remind you of the patterns.)

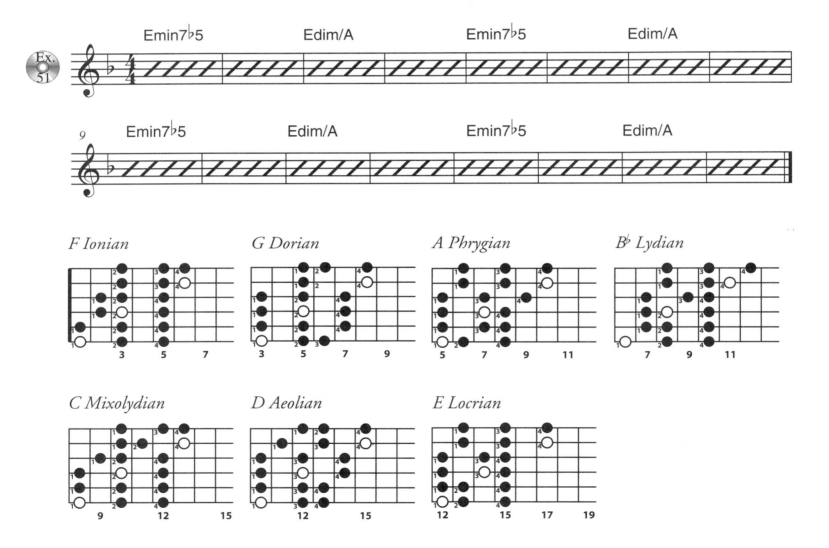

Your knowledge of the fretboard just increased significantly. Doesn't it feel good? Spend some time jamming along with this track.

Harmonic Minor (Root Position)

The harmonic minor scale is one of the most unique-sounding scales. It is used in metal, fusion, Latin, Spanish, neo-classical, and world music. In this lesson, we'll be checking out this scale and learning some licks.

THE A HARMONIC MINOR SCALE AND TIPS ON CREATING PATTERNS

The harmonic minor scale is not much different from an Aeolian scale. The only difference is that the 7th note of harmonic minor is one fret higher than the 7th note of the Aeolian scale. That's it. The distance between the flat 6th and the regular 7th is what gives this scale such a unique sound and feel on the guitar fretboard. The formula for this scale is: whole–half–whole–whole–half–whole plus half–half.

A Harmonic Minor

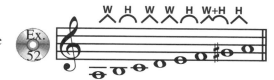

To the right is the A Harmonic Minor scale starting from the A on the 5th fret of the 6th string. Remember, it's just like the Aeolian scale until you get to the 7th scale tone, which is a half step higher. In addition, watch out for the stretch on the 2nd string from the 6th fret to the 9th fret. Practice this scale ascending and descending. Sounds cool, doesn't it?

A Harmonic Minor

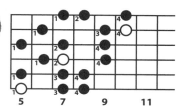

Some of the chords that go with this scale are A Minor, E7, and Amin(Maj7).

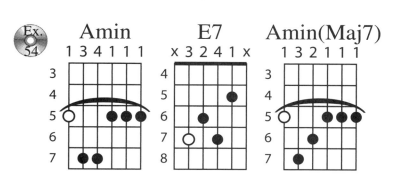

Now, we're going to learn a more musical way to practice scales. Just running scales up and down can get pretty boring. Focusing on the 6th string for the moment, let's learn different variations as alternatives to the standard low note (5th fret), mid note (7th fret), and high note (8th fret) up the scale. We can play these notes in any order we want. For instance, we could play low note, high note, mid note; or mid note, low note, high note; or maybe high note, low note, mid note; there are many different variations. By practicing scales in a musical way, you'll end up improvising in a musical way.

A Harmonic Minor Pattern

Now, we'll take a look at a pattern called *low–high–mid* (1st note, 3rd note, 2nd note). We're going to play this pattern on all the strings, ascending and descending. But first, play the scale straight up and down to hear how it sounds.

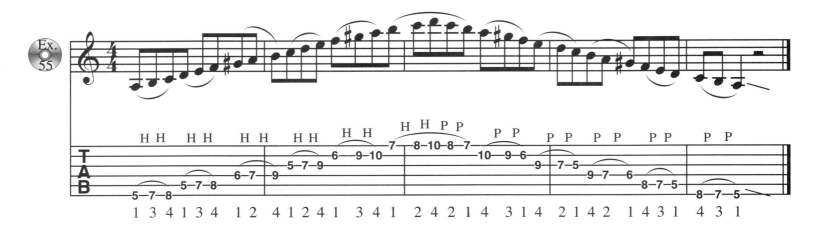

Not bad, but a little boring, right? Now, let's try it with a different flavor, using the low–high–mid pattern. Play it slowly at first, and watch out for the stretch on the B string. Once you are comfortable, increase the tempo.

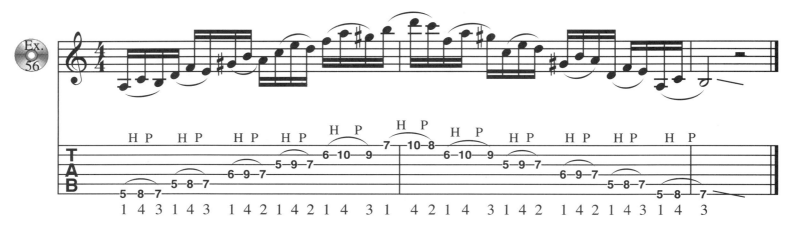

Take your time getting used to this scale with the root on the 6th string.

Starting the A Harmonic Minor Scale on the 5th String

Now, let's learn a harmonic minor scale pattern starting on the 5th string. This is basically the same shape as the 6th-string pattern, but when we get to the B string, we'll have to move the shape from the previous pattern up one fret—that's the only difference. Note that the stretch on the B string in the root-6 pattern is now on the high-E string. Give it a try.

Now, we're going to take a look at a variation of this scale similar to the low–high–mid pattern we learned before. Our new variation is *mid–high–low* (2nd note–3rd note–1st note). It's a little challenging to play the scale like this, but it sounds cool. As I said before, please try some of these variations yourself. Start off slow, with the *legato* technique, then try it a bit faster.

> ### Legato
> Legato means smooth and connected. On the guitar, any technique that involves sounding a note without picking a string (hammer-ons, pull-offs, tapping, etc.) creates a legato sound.

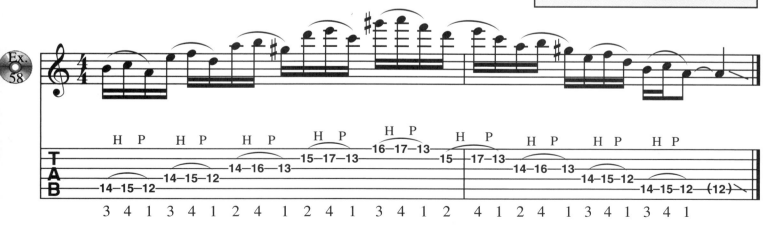

COOL SOLO LICK (A HARMONIC MINOR)

It's time to learn a cool lick using the 5th-string root A Harmonic Minor scale from the last lesson. The lick includes a string-skipping pattern to give it some flair and interval shock value. We're also going to be cramming six notes (two triplets) into the time of four eighth notes, so this is going to be pretty fast.

Now, try the following lick. Watch for the string-skip from the 5th string to the 3rd string in measure 1, from the 4th string to the 2nd string in measure 2, and from the 3rd string to the 1st string in measure 2, as well. Additionally, watch the bend and vibrato on the last note. Try this example slowly at first, then give it a shot at a faster tempo.

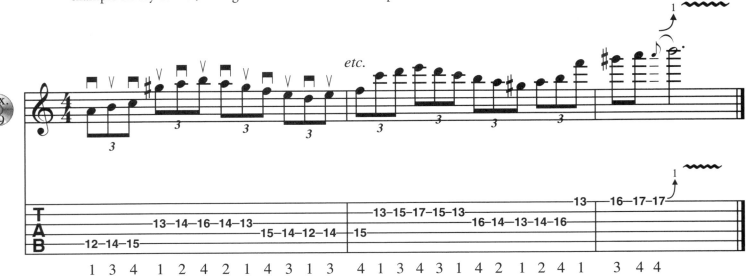

Now, try to make your own patterns and shapes from the scale. Also, keep in mind that nothing is wrong—it just hasn't been explored yet.

EXTRA HARMONIC MINOR SCALE PRACTICE

Practice Example No. 1

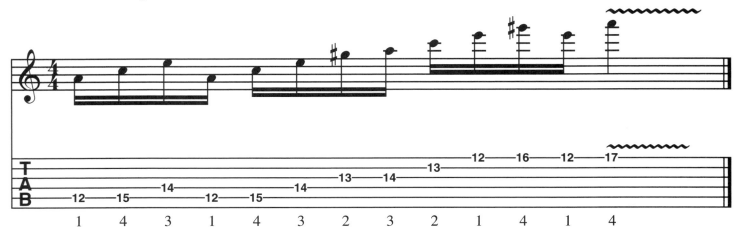

Practice Example No. 2

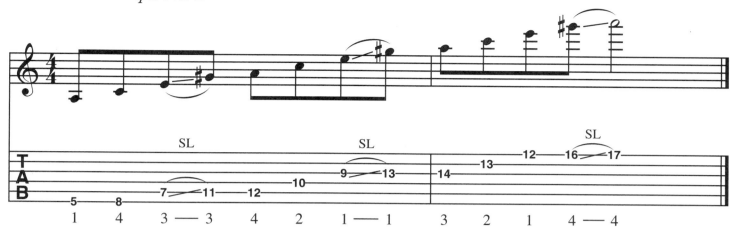

Practice Example No. 3

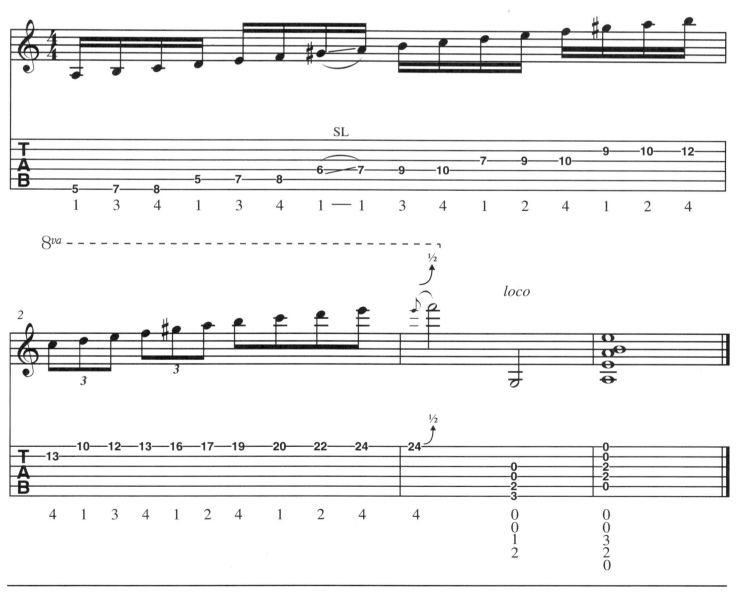

Melodic Minor (Root Position)

I used to hate this scale; but now that I know how to use it, I love it. I remember listening to certain solos from artists and wondering: What is that? Why can't I do that? What is that sound? It was because I foolishly dismissed the melodic minor scale. Well, I'm here to make sure you don't make the same mistake. Let's begin!

MELODIC MINOR FORMULA

Are you aware that you almost know this scale already? I'm sure you can play a major scale by now... Melodic minor has only one note different from the major scale: a ♭3. So the step formula for a melodic minor scale is: whole–half–whole–whole–whole–whole–half.

A Melodic Minor

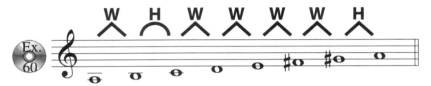

Now, lets's play the melodic minor shape below, ascending and descending. Notice the interesting major and minor sound.

A Melodic Minor
(6th-String Root)

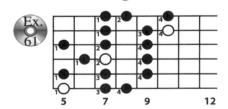

On the video, we'll play it again with a backing track using the chord Amin(Maj7). This is the first chord in the melodic minor family. Here we go.

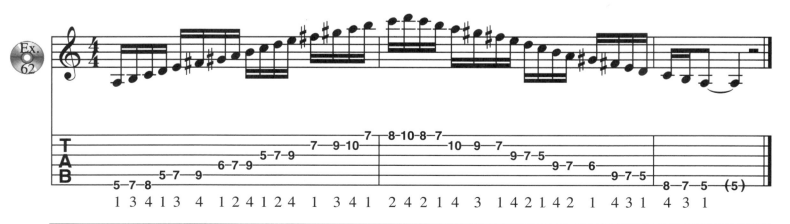

LOW-HIGH-MID PATTERN

Now, let's play the melodic minor scale with a low–high–mid variation (1st note–3rd note–2nd note). Go through it slowly at first, then try to play it fast, along with me, to the Amin(Maj7) backing track.

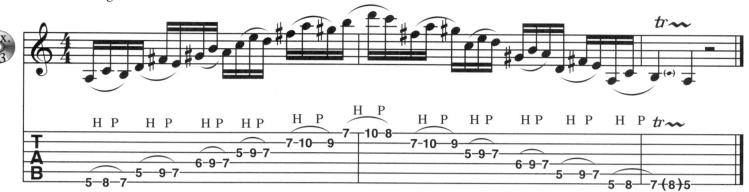

5TH-STRING ROOT A MELODIC MINOR

Now, we're going to learn the melodic minor scale starting from the 5th string. It is basically the same shape as the 6th-string version, with a change on the 2nd string. Play the entire scale, up and down.

*A Melodic Minor
(5th-String Root)*

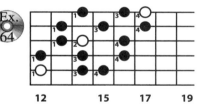

Now, on the video, I will play the scale over a backing track that uses the D7 chord, the fourth chord in A Melodic Minor. Hint: A lot of blues players are onto this little secret, and now so are you!

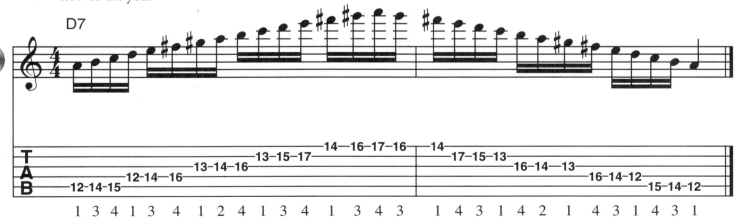

HIGH-LOW-MID-HIGH-MID-LOW PATTERN

Now, let's apply a high–low–mid–high–mid–low pattern to the 5th-string root A Melodic Minor scale. So the pattern is: 3rd note–1st note–2nd note–3rd note–2nd note–1st note on each string. Try that pattern slowly to make sure you've got it.

Notice the sixteenth-note triplet feel in the example below. On the video, I'll play this lick along with the backing track at 110 beats per minute.

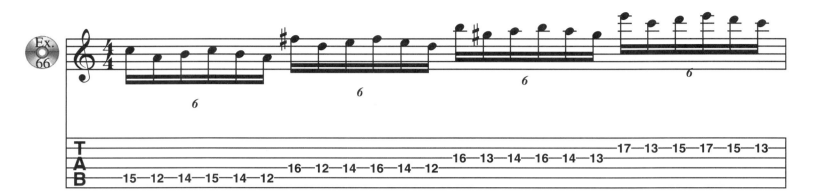

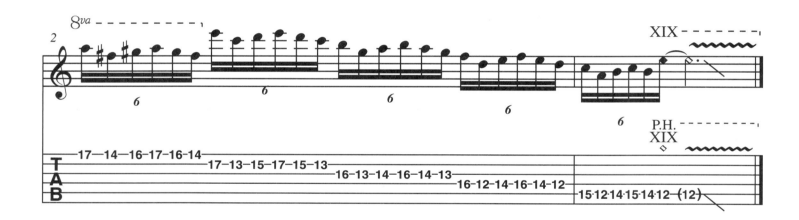

Make sure you can play these shapes in your sleep. Also, try coming up with your own variations on these patterns.

Modal Interchange

Just when you thought life was simple, everything changes. This lesson introduces you to *modal interchange*, which consists of moving modes around to achieve a new color or sound in your playing. There are some standard methods to do this, and we'll cover three of them. The practice section on page 41 covers three more examples. Basically, we need to find out what chords live in certain keys and be able to pivot from those chords into new perceived keys of the moment. This might sound confusing but really is not that bad. So let's dig in.

DEFINITION AND APPLICATION

As mentioned above, modal interchange is the process of moving scales around within a chord progression to achieve different tonalities and colors. In our warm-up example below, we have two chords: F#min and Asus2. We can assume the F#min is the vi chord in the key of A Major, and Asus2 is a fancy I chord in the same key—this is pretty much the standard approach. (The I, IV, and V chords are major in the key; the ii, iii, and vi are minor; and the vii is diminished.)

(Note: Play all examples in this section twice. Perform the scales ascending and descending the first time through, and then improvise the second time.)

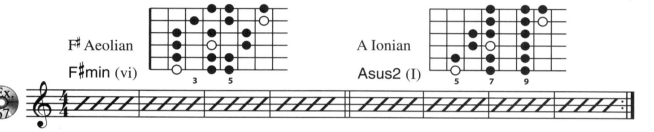

Easy, right? Now, let's assume F#min is the ii chord in the key of E Major. That would make Asus2 the IV chord. So, basically, instead of assuming we have the vi and I in A Major, we're thinking now that we have the ii and IV in E Major. This is totally legal because these two chords exist in both keys. Now, in our new key of E Major, we're going to play F# Dorian over F#min and A Lydian over Asus2.

In the following example, each scale is outlined; what you have to do is practice with a backing groove to get used to this change. It will sound a little funky to your ears, but you'll get used to it. First, just play the scales over the groove, and then try your hand at some improvisation.

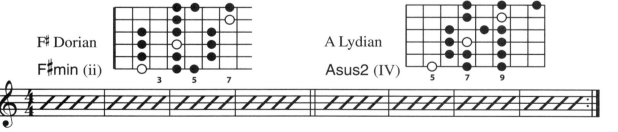

Also note that we could just use the E Ionian scale over the whole progression and it would work fine, because these scales are all from the same family. Practice and get used to this change before you attempt the next lesson.

Substituting Different Tonal Colors

I hope you took your time with that last example. These things cannot be rushed. The next one includes the same chords—the only difference is that the A chord, which we voiced before as Asus2, will now be A7. We have to figure out what key has F#min as the iii chord and A7 as the V chord. The process of elimination takes us to D Major, which has F#min as the iii chord and A7 as the V chord. So, that means we can play F# Phrygian over F#min and A Mixolydian over A7. This gives us a noticeable Middle-Eastern sound over the changes, especially on the F#min. On the video, I play up and down the scales along with the backing track, then, the second time around, I improvise. Practice this concept yourself along with the separate jam track on your DVD.

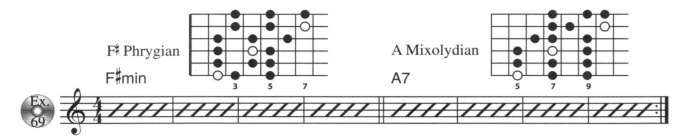

Notice the different colors created by using modal interchange? Work with the sound above for a while, get used to the positions, and then try using the D Ionian scale over the whole chord progression.

Implying Two Key Changes

It's time for a tricky example. Our chords remain the same as above, but we're going to look at each as being from a different key. We're going to think of F#min as the ii chord in the key of E Major, which means we'll play F# Dorian over that chord. Unlike our previous examples where the chords were from the same key (thus allowing a particular Ionian scale to be played over them), we're now going to think of A7 as being the V chord in D Major. So, we will play A Mixolydian over that chord. To sum up: The first key of E has four sharps. The second key of D has two sharps. When we switch to A Mixolydian, notice how the G-natural and D-natural notes really stand out, as they were sharped in the previous key.

Now, play up and down the scales, and then practice improvising to the separate jam track on your DVD.

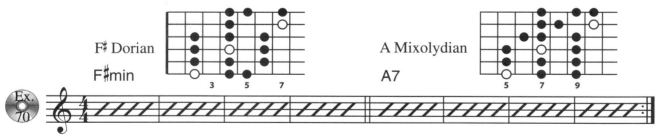

Notice the new sound colors? Here, they're even stronger than with previous examples, as they're implying two key changes. Work very hard to master this simple idea. When you're done, try the practice examples on the next page.

Extra Modal Interchange Practice

Practice Example No. 1

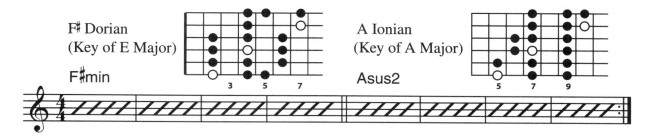

F# Dorian (Key of E Major) — F#min — A Ionian (Key of A Major) — Asus2

Practice Example No. 2

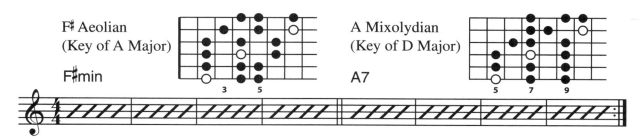

F# Aeolian (Key of A Major) — F#min — A Mixolydian (Key of D Major) — A7

Practice Example No. 3

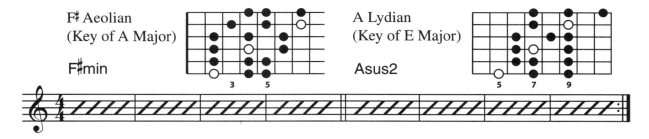

F# Aeolian (Key of A Major) — F#min — A Lydian (Key of E Major) — Asus2

Creative Use of Pentatonic Scales

So, you thought there was only one way to use the pentatonic scale, did you? In this lesson, I will show you three new ways of moving pentatonic shapes around to create new sounds. Many players assume you have to use the pentatonic traditionally, but there are many secrets hidden inside this five-note scale. We will look at pentatonic Boxes 3, 4, and 1 being used in a non-traditional method.

BOX 3 BUILT ON THE ROOT

Our first exercise superimposes Box 3 where Box 1 usually goes (in other words, if you are in the key of A Minor, start Box 3 on the 5th fret of the 6th string, where you would normally start Box 1). This is a cool way of getting new sounds out of your old pentatonic friend. Traditionally, you would play Box 1 over A Minor, and you would sound like millions of other players. We don't want that!

When we build Box 3 starting on our root in A Minor, we get the following scale degrees: 1–2–4–5–$\flat$7. That sounds harmless enough, right? First, just play the scale up and down, then play along with the A Minor jam track on the DVD.

Notice the new sound? By using Box 3 in this way, we're implying the key of G Major instead of the traditional C Major.

Get used to playing Box 3 over a minor chord. You might find your fingers want to move back to the old way, but fight this urge!

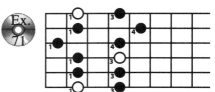

Box 3 Built on the Root

BOX 4 BUILT A HALF STEP BELOW THE ROOT

In the next exercise, we'll learn a new pentatonic shape to play over a major 7th chord. The chord we'll be using is EMaj7. Traditionally, guitarists play major pentatonic Box 2 on E and call it a day. That's boring! Let's learn a new way. Play major pentatonic Box 4 starting one half step below the root (on E$\flat$).

Notice this shape gives us scale degrees 7, 9, 3, 5, and 13. These all have a cool relationship to the chord.

We've discovered a totally new sound to use over a major 7th chord. Now, improvise with this scale over the jam track on the DVD.

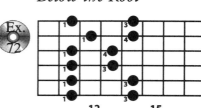

Box 4 Built a Half Step Below the Root

BOX 1 BUILT A WHOLE STEP ABOVE THE ROOT

This concept involves playing the regular minor pentatonic Box 1 up a whole step from the minor chord you're playing. So, in this example, we'll play a B Minor Pentatonic over an A Minor chord. Check out the scale diagram below, with the correct roots indicated. Play the scale, both ascending and descending.

Box 1 Built a Whole Step
Above the Root

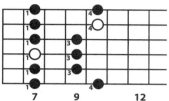

By playing this shape one step up from the root, the resulting intervals are a 9th, 4th, 5th, natural 6th, and root. A Dorian flavor is implied because of the natural 6th—a very cool sound (though it might take some time for your ears to get used to). Practice the scale, and then try your hand at improvising over the A Minor jam track on your DVD.

CONGRATULATIONS!

You have completed *Dave Martone's Serious Shred: Advanced Scales.* If you've been practicing and reading carefully, you have gained some important skills and knowledge. Be sure to check out the other books in the Serious Shred series.

Appendix:
Pentatonic and Blues Scale Box Shapes

Note: All minor scales are demonstrated in the key of A Minor, and all major scales are in the relative key of C Major.

MINOR PENTATONIC BOXES

○ = Root

1

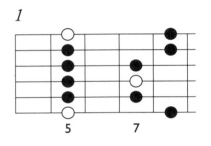

2

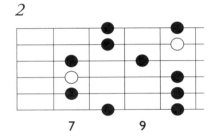

3

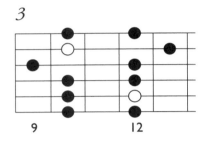

4

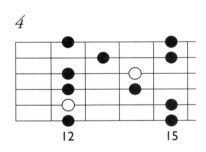

5

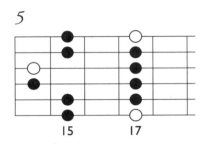

MAJOR PENTATONIC BOXES

1

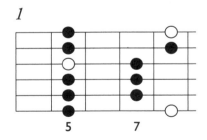

2

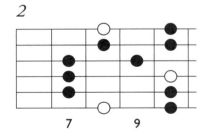

3

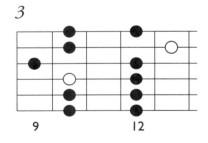

4

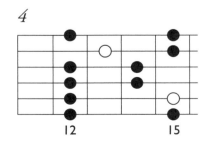

5

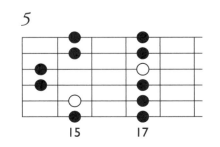

MINOR BLUES SCALE BOXES

1

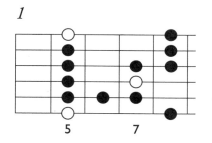

2

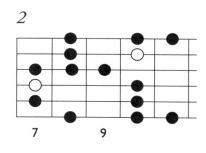

3

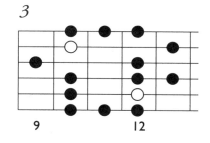

4

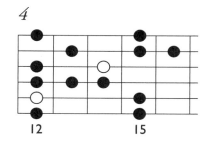

5

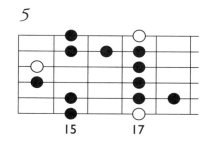

MAJOR BLUES SCALE BOXES

1

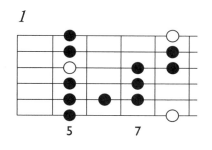

2

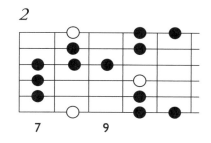

3

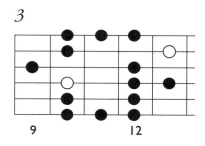

4

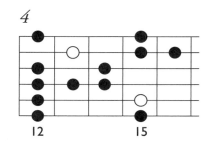

5

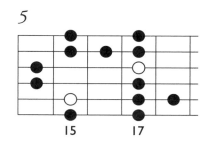

Guitar TAB Glossary

TABLATURE EXPLANATION

READING TABLATURE: Tablature illustrates the six strings of the guitar. Notes and chords are indicated by the placement of fret numbers on a given string(s).

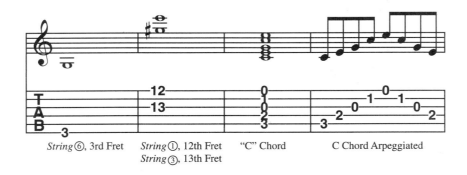

String ⑥, 3rd Fret   String ①, 12th Fret   "C" Chord   C Chord Arpeggiated
String ③, 13th Fret

BENDING NOTES

HALF STEP: Play the note and bend string one half step.*

WHOLE STEP: Play the note and bend string one whole step.

PRE-BEND AND RELEASE: Bend the string, play it, then release to the original note.

 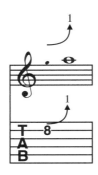 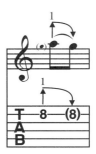

RHYTHM SLASHES

STRUM INDICATIONS: Strum with the indicated rhythm.

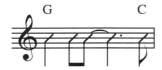

* A half step is the smallest interval in Western music; it is equal to one fret. A whole step equals two frets.

ARTICULATIONS

HAMMER-ON: Play the lower note, then "hammer on" to a higher note with another finger. Only the first note is picked.

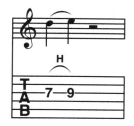

PULL-OFF: Play the higher note, then "pull off" to a lower note with another finger. Only the first note is picked.

LEGATO SLIDE: Play a note and slide to the following note. (Only the first note is picked).

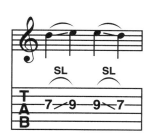

PALM MUTE: The note or notes are muted with the palm of the picking hand by lightly touching the string(s) near the bridge.

ACCENT: Notes or chords are to be played with added emphasis.

DOWNSTROKES AND UPSTROKES: Notes or chords are to be played with either a downstroke (◼) or upstroke (V) of the pick.